DREAM HOMES

HouseBeautiful

DREAM HOMES

INTIMATE HOUSE TOURS & DAZZLING SPACES

Caroline Picard

HEARST
books

contents

1

A SPREAD IN THE COUNTRY

....

A family estate, an antiques-filled farmhouse, or a mountain getaway: Walking into a provincial home feels as refreshing as the crisp air outside it. These rural retreats live up to the splendor of their surroundings with wholesome touches that get back to the land.

A Lake Tahoe town in California is the setting for a home with a beguiling outdoor living room with ample opportunities for entertaining in refreshingly crisp fresh air.

a secret garden

A surprise awaits around every corner on textile artist and entrepreneur Rebecca Vizard's Louisiana property. The grounds border scenic Lake Bruin, but the gardens' magical aura evoke somewhere even more fantastical.

LEFT: The entryway connects the living areas with Vizard's studio and doubles as a flower-arranging room. "The vine on the ceiling crept in several years ago, and I decided to leave it, even after my gardener mistakenly killed it," Vizard says. "It is beautiful—why not?" RIGHT: The storybook garden shed mimics an equally quaint post office Vizard spotted in Seaside, Florida. She takes breaks from designing pillows for her business, B. Viz Design, by tending to the fenced vegetable plot.

The designer, her husband Michael, and their dogs, Lucille and Lou, steer their 1972 Correct Craft through a grove of trees.

FOLLOWING PAGES: Wide cypress boards with distressed red paint surround the barn-like living room. Slipcovered seating washes easily— perfect for when guests bring over their dogs. Vizard designed the "cork-de-lier" overhead herself.

Vizard trained fig ivy to envelop the entrance to her exquisitely detailed home, located less than a mile from the Mississippi River.

TOP LEFT: In the dining room, a nineteenth-century Russian ecclesiastical textile hangs next to an antique French hutch purchased in Baton Rouge.

TOP RIGHT: Vizard's grandfather originally bought the rural property in the 1950s. "I garner a lot of creativity from this place," she says. "When I get stumped on a pillow design, I go outside and garden for a few minutes, and soon I come back inside with a better idea."

RIGHT: A stay in a tiny room at the Hotel Verneuil in Paris inspired the cozy guest bedroom. Cubbyholes on either side of the vintage Kazakh suzani headboard provide spots for books and water (plus outlets for charging devices).

Tucked within the cypress trees, the dock acts as an extension of the living space. "We love to cook down here and swim every day," Vizard says. "I usually wash my hair in the lake all summer."

" I wanted a New Orleans–style farmhouse, lake house, and hunting lodge, all in one.

—REBECCA VIZARD

heirloom material

For a New Jersey farmhouse that's welcomed home five generations of the same family, Jeffrey Bilhuber rejected scrubbed white rooms in favor of an invigorating lime-green, mandarin-orange, and royal-purple palette. With a riot of color from the root cellar to the rafters, this estate's story is just getting started.

In the former living room, Bilhuber created a reception hall with a big, comfortable sofa and a vintage rattan chair as the welcoming committee. A pair of paintings by Dan Walsh provides a sneak peak of the saturated colors to come.

The silo at the still-active Dunwalke Farm in Far Hills, New Jersey, bears its initials. Cows, pigs, sheep, goats, and a pack of hounds also call it home.

Built for a farm tenant years ago, the original homestead has since grown to accommodate the current owner's great-grandfather's descendants. Architect John Heyrich found additional space by joining several outbuildings together into sprawling home.

FOLLOWING PAGES: Checked curtains set the mood for the fearlessly decorated master bedroom. Bilhuber painted the window muntins green so they would blend in with the bucolic landscape beyond.

"I'm a pushover for gingham curtains.

—JEFFREY BILHUBER

pocket of paradise

Getting away is as easy as walking out the backdoor at Shelley Johnstone Paschke's family home in Lake Forest, Illinois. The designer went all-in on a Hollywood Regency–inspired poolhouse used April all the way until November as a splash zone and breezy dining spot.

Architect Austin DePree designed the backyard poolhouse, which the residents also use as an outdoor living room. The structure houses changing rooms and storage for pool toys.

The vintage chaises' cushions match happy pink towels inspired by a hotel in Capri.

Both dinner parties and breakfast are served outside on fine china. "If I like something, I use it, and I don't worry about anything breaking," Paschke says.

The 1950s Dutch Colonial Revival house in the Chicago suburbs was built by a man who was inspired by his home in a David Adler–designed co-op.

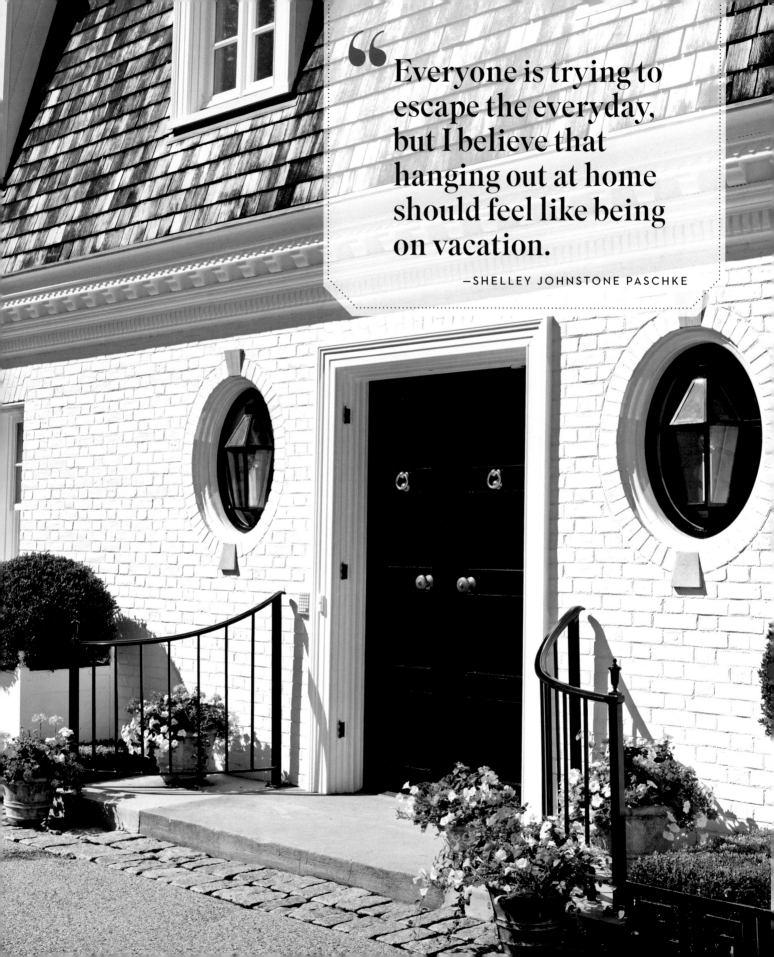

" Everyone is trying to escape the everyday, but I believe that hanging out at home should feel like being on vacation.

—SHELLEY JOHNSTONE PASCHKE

farm fresh

Set on a 380-acre spread in Tennessee, a new home designed by Barbara Westbrook gains all the charm of an old-timer. Patinated country furniture and woven baskets throughout give the walls wisdom beyond their years.

An apron sink and antique grape-drying baskets warm up
a sun-drenched kitchen with twelve-foot ceilings. A hand-
applied glaze on the cabinets adds a timeworn aura.

Framed with a pine mantel, the fireplace provides a glowy focal point.
The idyllic landscape painting above sits between tin sconces.

"It's a farm, we didn't want anything *too* fancy!

—BARBARA WESTBROOK

With a restoration in its near future, the property's original horse barn will shine brightly once again.

A ceiling painted haint blue—the traditional color for Southern porches—shades the outdoor seating area. Classic wicker and pillows in a homey plaid beckon guests outside for views of the rolling green hills.

a warm embrace

Old-house features—low ceilings, abundant fireplaces—meet some unexpected ones—red lacquer, lattice wallpaper—in a Vermont getaway designed by Ramsay Gourd. Put it all together, and there's a room for every mood.

A wing chair in a sitting area just off the kitchen provides a comfy fireside seat. A peekaboo fabric on the inside breaks up the frame's expanse.

To avoid a toile with any dated impressions, Gourd designed his own, mixed with an ikat-like pattern. The library's high-gloss, candy apple walls "envelope you like a big, energetic hug."

Gourd turned to local Vermont soapstone for counters that will stain and age over the years. "That's part of its beauty," he says. The crimson back door provides another contrast to creamy Shaker-style cabinets.

A spool bed handmade from solid pine provides the focal point for the restful master bedroom. The wallpaper echoes its curvaceous shapes.

"
Sometimes you want to feel refreshed, and sometimes you want to be embraced.

—RAMSAY GOURD

seeking new heights

At a treetop retreat near Lake Tahoe, designer Matt O'Dorisio skips the ski-lodge cliché in favor of an elevated chalet with attitude. This one sings right to the reclaimed-wood rafters.

The refined dining area remains dinner party–ready with a custom plank table that seats fourteen.

Tucked in the middle of the house, a stairwell nook became a cozy games corner. The drawers under the banquette provide storage for pieces and puzzles.

Pullman train cars inspired the curtained bunk beds in the boys' bedroom. Kids' rooms can take color, O'Dorisio says, so he doused it with a playful green, rather than a classic knotty pine.

FOLLOWING PAGES: Majestic pine trees as far as the eye can see provide the backdrop to the bluestone patio. Contemporary teak, married with traditional wicker, feels like an extension of the décor inside.

southern soul

After eyeing it for years, Matthew Carter bought his 1928 Greek Revival in Lexington, Kentucky, the day it went on the market. With a mix of proper Southern furnishings and finds from afar, the timeless yet fresh interiors now match up with a classically landscaped garden.

A restrained palette of green and white connects the extensive gardens. Carter hangs potted ferns from the trees every spring, making the plants appear to float in midair.

PRECEDING PAGES, LEFT: Stained floors punctuate the breakfast room. Carter's partner, architect Brent Bruner, added the floor-to-ceiling windows during a remodel. RIGHT: A mix of high and low artworks—a Picasso lithograph, Mexican folk art from the streets of Tulum—cluster around an antique Italian mirror in the living room.

The bluestone patio hosts guests for cocktail hour. Visitors then follow a pathway of local Kentucky limestone over to the pergola, and finally to the dinner table under the sycamore tree.

> " Being instinctual has always
> worked for me. I go with my gut.
>
> —MATTHEW CARTER

manor of the hour

No room is off-limits for the young children living in a nineteenth-century farmhouse in upstate New York. "This is a real home, not a showpiece," says designer Ashley Whittaker, who looked to classic English estates for inspiration. Bolstered with brave color and pattern, nothing's off-limits in the design, either.

Playful chairs with curlicues act as the foil to an heirloom dining table and china cabinet.
Missing sections in the Venetian mirror were filled with silvered wood.

FOLLOWING PAGES: Comfy seating
and refreshments draw guests
outdoors. "It's a rural farmhouse,"
Whittaker states. "You can't do
precious."

An underutilized downstairs passageway now acts as "the family Starbucks,"
where they sip coffee and check social media by the window seat. The nook's
five different prints draw on repeating colors to create a sense of cohesion.

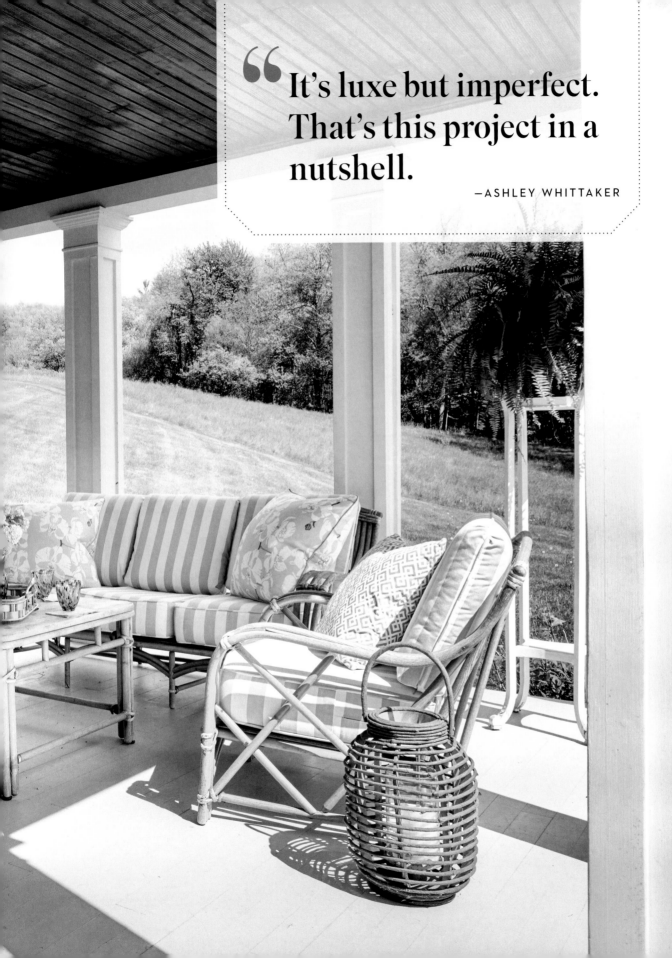

"It's luxe but imperfect. That's this project in a nutshell.

—ASHLEY WHITTAKER

2

ON THE WATER

Lapping waves and cool breezes turn these water-front abodes into true paradises. Lazy days at the lake or the beach beckon for homes like these.

A sun-dappled deck overlooking one of Ontario's Muskoka Lakes sits right amongst the swaying pines, with plush outdoor sofas for breaks from swimming and boating.

law of the lake

Geometric pattern and storybook style lay the groundwork for a cabin campground deep in New York's Adirondacks. It's rugged but never rough at this wooded wonderland, designed by Anthony Baratta.

Right from the entryway, the exuberant front door and French painted clock telegraph the color palette: woodsman-y reds and the blues of the Adirondack sky and water.

A hanging daybed on a screened-in porch provides a breezy bug-free spot to lounge.

A blue-canopied Budsin Wood Craft electric launch, which cuts the water as silently as a canoe, is the crown jewel of the boathouse.

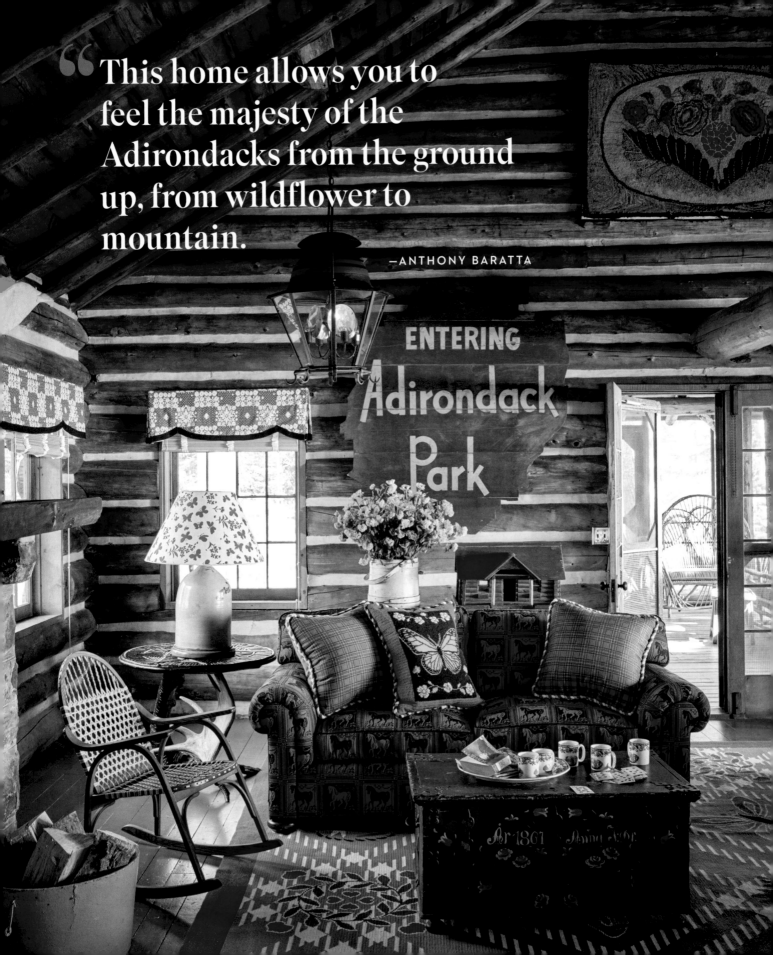

"This home allows you to feel the majesty of the Adirondacks from the ground up, from wildflower to mountain.

—ANTHONY BARATTA

A secluded lake in the Adirondack Mountains serves as the backdrop for the nearly 10-acre camp. "This family compound is a classic, with all the charm and beauty of cabins on a lake in the woods," designer Anthony Baratta says of the dockside retreat. "It doesn't have the Gilded Age formality of 'great camps' that were fully staffed for very short summers."

Log walls set the baseline for the rhythmic colors and patterns in the Summer House, a good hike and woodland creek away from the all-weather Winter House.

The owner, a wildlife photographer, raises butterflies in a sanctuary garden filled with native, pollinator-friendly plants.

A fire pit ringed with wine-barrel Adirondack chairs invites stargazers and marshmallow roasters out on summer nights. The designer padded the lean-to with a ground-level mattress and plump pillows for further lounging.

through the looking glass

Walk into any room at decorator Anne Hepfer's Canadian cottage and there's no forgetting its location. Every space in the dream getaway is oriented toward the beauty of Ontario's Lake Joseph beyond, with smart furnishings and eye-catching treasures in between.

PRECEDING PAGES: A twenty-foot-high wall of windows ushers sweeping vistas into the living room. Wide-plank pine wallboards and flooring balance the vast proportions.

Unlike railings, frameless glass panels shield the deck from wind without obscuring the gorgeous sunsets.

Hepfer asked the stonemason to leave the lichen intact on the fireplace's locally quarried granite for character. The taller, shallower Rumford-style design radiates more heat into the living room.

FOLLOWING PAGES: Breezes enter the breakfast nook via awning windows that crank open. A pair of marble-topped tables bisect the banquette for easy access in and out.

" You gaze directly out onto the swaying pines; it's almost like you're in a tree house.

—ANNE HEPFER

racing stripes

A lovely Wisconsin lake is front and center at a weekend house layered with loads of patterns. Summer Thornton employed swathes of stripes and saturated aquas for an interior with views just as pretty as the peninsula outside.

Green-and-blue stripes add zing to the covered porch's floor, echoing the zigzags on the playful bistro chairs.

Horizontal blue stripes mimic the adjacent wall's planking in a hallway outside the master suite.

A white headboard provides a restful respite in the master bedroom. The grass-cloth-covered walls showcase the Balinese artwork hanging over the bed.

FOLLOWING PAGES: In the kitchen, custom red interiors peek out from the brass pendants hanging above the island. Oak-clad ceilings warm up a spacious downstairs built for entertaining.

> "The more colors you use, the better they go together.

—SUMMER THORNTON

turn of the tide

With the sea rushing in and out of the reinforced pilings below, this former fisherman's shack in Provincetown, Massachusetts, is the real deal. Working with quarters as tight as a ship, Frank Roop transforms a seaside cottage into dreamy getaway.

Authentic portholes from a marine supplier add light to the kitchen. The honed granite countertops give the appearance of slate but with added durability.

Roop added a vintage root table to the living room "so it doesn't feel pretentious." Keeping the furniture low-slung and on legs creates the illusion of higher ceilings.

A local fisherman tied off the stair's rope railings. An intricate sailor's knot tops the newel post.

The four-foot-deep banquette acts like a giant bed for TV watching. The old-fashioned roll-up curtains actually hide modern solar shades that go down at the push of the button.

boho breeze

A Tudor home on the New Jersey shore looks a whole lot younger than its 100 years with an influx of wallpaper and plants. Colleen Bashaw pulls out her best decorating tricks for a beach house that goes with the wind.

Nautical brass in the kitchen—including on the custom scalloped hood—nods to the home's location. Encasing the refrigerator with cerused oak makes the appliance feel more like a piece of furniture.

FAR LEFT: The nearby breakfast room features the same turquoise as the kitchen island, this time on the window muntins. Rattan elements break up the bold blue.

Spas served as the inspiration for a master bathroom enveloped in palm-leaf wallpaper. The undulating pattern on the mosaic-tile floor mimics the ebbing waves outside.

FOLLOWING PAGES: Woven textures mingle with pops of color in the richly layered living room. Bashaw re-covered the wingback chairs in a gold-leaf ficus print because "They came in plain linen, and I believe you just can't have plain linen in your living room!"

the gold standard

Marshall Watson and Kate Reid
aimed for comfort and timeless
sophistication in a Lake Michigan
beach house in need of a refresh.
With imaginative textile pairings,
this is summer at the lake by
the pros.

Watson painted the formerly blue exterior a custom coach-house green and white. By using two colors, "The house now looks added onto, and it fits so much better into the landscape."

PRECEDING PAGES: "Yellow is the color of light and fire—it emanates warmth," Watson says. In the breakfast room, gold-infused tones on the chairs, wallpaper, and curtains surround an inviting limed-oak table.

Bird prints from the owner's collection hang above a painted bench upholstered in a bright green.

FOLLOWING PAGES: In the master bedroom, scalloped flanges on the
roller shades lend old-world charm. The faux-bamboo headboard
was created from two antique twin-size beds.

"Every room in this house has an amazing view. You feel like you're on the upper deck of a ship.

—MARSHALL WATSON

funky fresh

Fabulous vintage finds set the tone at a vacation home on South Carolina's Kiawah Island. Tasked with giving an early '90s showhouse new life, Angie Hranowsky drew on a few surprising gems, including some nostalgic throwback furniture.

Gorgeous hand-painted wallpaper from the 1920s didn't quite stretch from floor to ceiling in the dining room, but chair rails and crown moldings fudge the distance. The curtains add a "sun-kissed" palette of pinks and yellows.

When Hranowsky found the modern abstract fabric for the dining room curtains, something clicked. "I loved the idea of pairing an old-fashioned, antique wallpaper with a contemporary, painterly fabric," she says.

The white leather chaise in the master bedroom dates to the '80s and served as the starting point for the room's tranquil vibes. A coral silk lining peeks out from behind sand-colored linen curtains.

"Vintage furniture helps a project feel original and fresh.

—ANGIE HRANOWSKY

Pops of fuchsia and plum on the study's pillows and custom lampshade warm up the smoky amethyst on the walls and ceiling.

Swimmers in the backyard lap pool can take breaks in the shaded gazebo.

The designer spotted the living room's 1980s peach slipper chairs outside a consignment shop and kept the existing fabric. A silk screen above the mantel adds an extra punch of orange.

Vintage chairs sidle up to a round table in the breakfast room. The quirky chandelier doubles as a spot to clip personal mementos.

The graphic print on the living room's curtains reappears throughout the first floor.

shored up

After Hurricane Sandy ravaged a 1926 Shingle-style home on the Jersey Shore, Joe Lucas helped his sailor client start afresh on a brand-new build. The blank canvas lent itself to his nautical leanings, with rope, jute, seagrass, and teak leading the way. It didn't hurt that the new higher siting also came with better views of the bay.

"'No white kitchens' is a rule for me," Lucas says. Punchy indigo and Moroccan tiles that "don't feel too beachy" add grounding color to the cook space.

The designer's family yacht is tied up near the home; Lucas grew up in the beach town and his parents still live nearby.

Spending the winter months in this full-time residence necessitated a cozy spot. A moody gray in the study glints platinum in the light, and wool on the tufted chair adds further warmth.

Shaped like the hull of a boat, the study's mahogany serving bar also features a copper insert for ice.
The watercolor hanging above partially inspired the room's palette.

Located at the center of the home, the dining room provides both a gathering space and design impact. Lucas used the fabric on the chairs as the jumping-off point for the main level's color scheme.

TOP LEFT: The pair of consoles in the living room survived the storm. "Their brass legs took on a kind of patina because of the water damage, but somehow the effect looks beautiful," Lucas says.

TOP RIGHT: A custom sofa fills the entire bayside end of the living room, with cozy corners for reading and watching sunsets.

BOTTOM: In the guest bedroom, tongue-and-groove paneling and closets incorporated in the rooflines evoke a vintage feel.

3

A GREAT OLD HOUSE

History is alive when longstanding homes receive makeovers for the ages. These celebrated estates prove that many things only get better with time.

The "ramble" behind an 1850s North Jersey home features classical urns, hellebores, and ferns across its five acres. The landscape was originally designed by the architect of New York's Central Park.

a page from bunny's book

Once the Cape Cod retreat of decorator and philanthropist Bunny Mellon, this twenty-six-acre waterfront compound hosted friends Jack and Jackie Kennedy before finding its current owners. Interior designer Kathryn M. Ireland tapped into the storied heiress's aesthetic for the quintessential New England retreat.

"It feels like a rambling cottage—charming, intimate, and totally unpretentious.

—KATHRYN M. IRELAND

PRECEDING PAGES: Situated on a private peninsula, the property's guesthouses, greenhouses, and outposts overlook the sound. Ireland used her own linens for the casual tablecloth and pillows on the beach cabana's porch.

A diamond pattern graces a hallway running through the house. "All the painted floors are original, and they are ravishing," the designer says.

Ireland likes incorporating a tiny bit of red into her rooms. The family room receives the hue via the tablecloth, pillows, and seat cushions.

Mellon loved a certain blue-gray shade, "almost like an English sky on a good day," says the designer who used the color in the guest bedroom. Ireland found the coronet in London years ago.

going monochrome

Moving into a short-term rental in Charleston, Jill Sharp Weeks didn't hesitate in making the 1740s home her own. Painting the entire interior one shade of gray unified the space—and created the perfect prelude to an epic courtyard garden.

> " You have no idea what's going to happen tomorrow. Why not live with extreme beauty today?
>
> —JILL SHARP WEEKS

New plantings and furniture transformed the once-neglected private garden into a lush oasis. The weeping willow shades a bubbling fountain.

String lights make the backyard patio feel like an extension of the adjacent dining room. "We often leave the huge wooden French doors open so that the room feels forty feet longer," Weeks says.

PRECEDING PAGES, LEFT: "Threading black throughout the house creates a sense of continuity," Weeks says of the dark accents across the rooms, including the master suite. RIGHT: The colonial-era home's petite scale didn't quite allow for symmetry in the bedroom, so Weeks overlapped the upholstered king-size headboard with one of the windows.

victorian sensibility

Asked to adorn this home in "mad old aunt décor," Martyn Lawrence Bullard took off running, outfitting an 1840s-era Rhode Island home with an eclecticism worthy of its Victorian heritage. His weapon of choice? Wallpaper, the height of fashion both then and now.

"*Mistake* is a bad word in decorating. Everybody has his or her own style and taste.

—MARTYN LAWRENCE BULLARD

The animated peacock blue in the kitchen is echoed in almost every room of the house.
A black granite counter tops the island.

RIGHT TOP: A wallcovering patterned with books wraps around the sitting room, setting the scene for rich reds and browns. "Decorating isn't just about creating a wonderful, comfortable space," Bullard explains. "It's about designing rooms that you feel good in, look good in, and love to be in."

RIGHT BOTTOM: Panels of agate-like paper hung incongruously add "Victorian frenzy" to the master bedroom.

PRECEDING PAGES: Bullard skipped beach clichés in favor of a layered living room with a black seagrass wallcovering. "That room is flooded with natural light, so I was able to get away with a darker scheme," he says.

The grand nineteenth-century home overlooking the Atlantic is "like something John Singer Sargent would have painted," Bullard says.

A row of lawn chairs aligns with the sparkling horizon beyond.

TOP LEFT: Inspired by Barbra Streisand's 1960s New York apartment, a paisley-covered bedroom features a cohesive thread of purple running throughout.

TOP RIGHT: Study prints of dragonflies and butterflies adorn a petite powder room. "Almost every room has a surprise, which makes this house so fun," Bullard says.

LEFT: Black trim and a ticking stripe accentuate the cozy eaves and dormer in a child's guest bedroom.

turning back time

Janie Molster's assignment: Showcase a storied
collection of artworks in a mid-1700s Virginia house,
itself a former museum piece until just a few years ago.
Straddling the line between respectful preservation
and a gutsy update for the present, the restoration
adds a new chapter to a never-ending story.

A consultation with a restoration specialist revealed that the banister and handrail in the narrow back stairwell date back even earlier than the three-hundred-year-old house.

Portraits by William and Mary de Leftwich Dodge, distant relatives of the owner, adorn a corner of the dining room. Floor-to-ceiling curtains in a charcoal linen velvet create drama among the antiques.

For the living room's gallery wall, Molster first laid out the paintings on the floor and used a ladder to "get perspective." Pumpkin silk taffeta curtains offset the waxed and polished wainscoting.

FOLLOWING PAGES: A contemporary chandelier and saturated colors balanced out the strength of the architecture in the study.

> "That's what creates cohesion— proportion and strength.

—JANIE MOLSTER

history, updated

In upstate New York, Anne Maxwell
Foster tapped her partner Suysel
dePedro Cunningham at design firm
Tilton Fenwick to assist with an update
of her 1850s house. On a time-honored
canvas, the duo pushed the boundaries
of their pattern-happy aesthetic further
than ever before.

The brass accents installed throughout the house remain unlacquered so they'll develop a patina over time.

Orange velvet covers a custom sofa in the Hudson Valley living room.
Ikat and tartan throw pillows round out the mix.

> "If the upholsterer doesn't ask whether we meant to put two very different fabrics together, we think, *Uh-oh, we didn't push it far enough.*
>
> —ANNE MAXWELL FOSTER

In the dining area, the rustic orange leather on the midcentury Italian chairs intensifies the poppy red of the wallpaper.

The designers embraced a country white kitchen so they could play with a bold floral wallpaper and Moroccan-tile backsplash. They had the wide floorboards painted to match.

The soldier's portrait in the wallpapered stair hall belonged to the previous owner. Maxwell Foster purchased the piece because "We didn't want him to leave his house."

"We've rarely painted a wall white—except, ironically, in Anne's living room, because the fireplace was amazing," dePedro Cunningham says. Two banquettes on either side of the faux-finished strié mantel maximize seating.

dash of the unexpected

"Every space benefits from an unpredictable moment," says Melissa Rufty, "Something that says, 'This isn't your grandmother's house.'" In a Georgian-style home in Louisiana once decorated by Mark Hampton, racy animal prints and unexpected shades almost call into question its eighty-plus-year history.

The designer kept the library's chocolate-brown hue, "an underrated color," but injected pinks and reds via a modern painting. Loads of textures—leather, faux fur, linen, velvet—cozy up the space.

The family's heirloom wicker fills the covered porch, grounded with jute rugs. An antique birdcage adds a dash of whimsy.

FOLLOWING PAGES: Silver-leaf floral wallpaper links the sunroom with the gardens outside. The owner's existing bergères get a vibrant update with lime-colored silk.

The existing curtains inspired the dining room's cantaloupe walls and an umber glaze steered the shade away from circus peanut orange. Rufty calls leopard-print fabric on the chairs the "high-heeled shoe in the room."

> "It's very much like music: You're subtly adjusting the bass and treble as you move through space.

—MELISSA RUFTY

going old school

Class is in session at a former one-room schoolhouse now filled with John Peixinho's treasures. A former teacher himself, the Rhode Island designer and antiques dealer sought out the modified building's circa-1794 charm, but added all the home's livable comforts—and ditched the rules, of course.

Antique Canton and Nanking export porcelain pop against the original milk paint inside the kitchen hutch. Peixinho uses the eighteenth- and nineteenth-century pieces regularly.

PRECEDING PAGES: A postwar-era bedroom on the ground floor became the dining area. The woven straw wallcovering "spans the range from casual to formal," he says, as well as the subtly mismatched mahogany side chairs.

The roof of a tumbledown chicken coop set atop tree-trunk columns shades the outdoor seating area. The wall-mounted wood flounder nods to the owner's surname, which means "little fish" in Portuguese.

Students once entered the landmark Peabody School via separate doors for boys and girls. Peixinho repainted the exterior with a period-appropriate red.

show stopper

The rooms in a 1920s Minneapolis colonial get a daring upgrade when former set decorator and stylist Janet Gridley works her theatrical magic. With the classic moldings as the backdrop, the family's flair for the contemporary finds its groove.

PRECEDING PAGES, LEFT: A blue as piercing as the Minnesotan skies graces a cabinet interior in the dining room. Repurposing the Milo Baughman table from the clients' previous residence worked beautifully with the elaborate spoon-carved millwork. RIGHT: Plants and ornate tables fill up the sunroom. "Even if you're starting from scratch, old pieces are grounding," Gridley explains. "You're never going to tire of them."

The home's traditional colonial façade fronts the surprisingly modern mix of treasures within.

After initially considering black, Gridley ultimately selected a mysterious blue for the cabinets in a spacious yet inviting kitchen. Brass light fixtures and hardware add glitz.

"The master bedroom, with its pale pinks and neutral tones, is like a world unto its own," the designer says. Monogrammed linens dress the bed.

A custom mural wallcovering along two sides of the room depicts blooming peonies.

FOLLOWING PAGES: Custom curved sofas follow the walls of the azure-painted library. Gridley paired animal prints with a deep palette throughout the house to "make a statement."

> "The classical architecture of the house was the dependable element that held it all together.

—JANET GRIDLEY

Illustrations cut from *Cabinet of Natural Curiosities*—the prized eighteenth-century natural history book—cover the powder room's walls.

In the living room, a blue linen-velvet covers the facing sofas. A coordinating bench pulls up to the vintage coffee table for extra seating during parties.

garden secrets

The roots of Michael Maher's North Jersey house run deep. The nineteenth-century gem shares an architect with Central Park in Calvert Vaux. More than 150 years later, this five-acre "ramble" still feels like a retreat from the city that lies just miles away.

PRECEDING PAGES: Rare botanical prints in a salon-style "hang" adorn striking blue walls in the dining room. The adjoining living room features an equally vibrant orange for contrast.

Even the well-used potting shed exudes charm. Maher installed an old zinc butler's-pantry sink atop iron sawhorses and an early twentieth-century mirror on decoratively painted walls.

Upstairs, Maher applied his love of color to a bedroom tucked in a dormer. Blues in plaids, stripes, and florals find their rhythm among the curves and hard lines.

Maher updated the deer-ravaged gardens with resistant hellebores and ferns. Classical urns and a Chinese chippendale chair nod to history.

> "The solarium's a
> great place to dance.
> See the heel dents
> in the floor?
>
> —MICHAEL MAHER

Outside, Gothic Revival dormers and a Second Empire mansard roof frame the eclectic exterior. Maher owns Calvert Vaux's original 1856 drawings for the house.

FAR RIGHT: Cutting through a pantry wall linked the breakfast nook with the rest of the house. An antique settee and 1940s French caned chairs encircle the hangout spot and homework station.

PRECEDING PAGES: An enlarged rug motif grounds the plant-filled solarium. The romantic landscape beyond pops against the oversize windows' black mullions.

A dozen mahogany dining room chairs swap out for eighteen bamboo ballroom seats when Maher hosts Sunday night dinner. "I have a big family, and everyone's welcome," he says.

4

A CHIC CITY PLACE

....

Urban confines place a premium on space, but these metropolitan homes never come up short on style. Petite pied-à-terre or towering town-house, city living never looked so plush.

Deep blue grasscloth walls envelop a sitting room in a Beverly Hills family home. Block-print cushions and swing-arm lamps enhance the cozy nook.

on the a-list

Ricky Strauss is a storyteller by trade. The movie executive works on some of Hollywood's greatest hits, and his penchant for narrative smartly informed the glamorous update of his 1930s Hollywood Regency home.

A hand-applied gold wall treatment in the dining room lends itself to displaying art and showcasing Strauss's frequently used fine china.

A blue "bedroom in the sky" uses built-ins to create a cozy cove for sleeping. Wall-to-wall carpeting absorbs sound—helpful when Sunset Boulevard lies less than a mile away.

PRECEDING PAGES: The living room's Scandinavian leather chairs have followed the owner from home to home as part of his "greatest hits" collection. A bowl on the coffee table previously belonged to Marilyn Monroe.

Animal prints—one of Strauss's favorite motifs—pop in a bar area already lacquered with green automotive paint. "It's a painstaking process," he says about the lacquered room he inherited. "If I didn't have to live through the trouble of creating one here, all the better."

> " I believe in a strictly authentic narrative at home— everything in my space is there for a reason.

—RICKY STRAUSS

glam squad

When a single mom with two young daughters requested a feminine makeover for her new Park Avenue pad, Sara Story decided to leave pink in the closet. Lacquered walls, lush fabrics, and flirty purples do the job just as well.

JAMES TURRELL
A RETROSPECTIVE

The Lucite-and-glass table in the dining area came with the apartment. Story paired it with Saarinen armchairs upholstered in a cotton velvet, and added three mirrors that "reflect all of the action."

A vibrant abstract of a stiletto by Ellen Berkenblit inspired the space's palette— and its POV: "sophisticated without any stiffness, so there's nothing off-limits or overly precious," Story says.

Mother-daughter bonding time happens in the master bath, clad in
Cararra marble. Built-in niches provide clever storage spaces.

per custom

No corner goes untouched in a stately
1930s Manhattan duplex, customized
by Frank de Biasi for a young family.
With both a contemporary streak and an
inviting warmth, this prewar apartment
checks off every box.

In Manhattan every closet counts. A newly created cubby under the stairs now works as a stash spot to keep sporting equipment out of sight.

The dining room's hand-painted silver wallpaper alludes to a lusher setting than the concrete jungle outside. De Biasi finished the silk taffeta curtains with old saris from a downtown shop for a fun, unexpected look.

"The library serves as the husband's man cave," the designer explains. A custom rug with a bold tribal motif laid the groundwork for the rich palette.

Tall shutters, folding flush with the wall, line the living room. "Curtains on that many windows would have made it look like a theater stage," de Biasi explains.

> "You can't pigeonhole it to a particular style, and that's good.
>
> —FRANK DE BIASI

day and night

After promising to keep a client's most beloved items, Melanie Turner combined the best of the old with the best of the new in an Atlanta home. With a thread of blue running throughout, everyone can get on board with this stylish redo.

"Grass cloth lends an earthy sense of comfort to a room, while black takes it to a new level of sophistication," Turner says of the wallcovering in the study.

PRECEDING PAGES: The lush velvet curtains and blue lacquer in the dining room feel "like you're wrapping yourself in a cloak," Turner says. "I'm a huge believer in creating rooms that have multiple uses, but this is a night room."

In the entry, a diamond-patterned design, more in keeping with the home's Georgian style, replaced subdued tile. Classic white walls work in the soaring space, and set up contrast with the darker rooms beyond.

FOLLOWING PAGES: Outfitting the kitchen island with more storage allowed Turner to ditch upper cabinets. A curved granite backsplash adds new interest and black mullions make the windowpanes look leaded, "an easy, inexpensive trick."

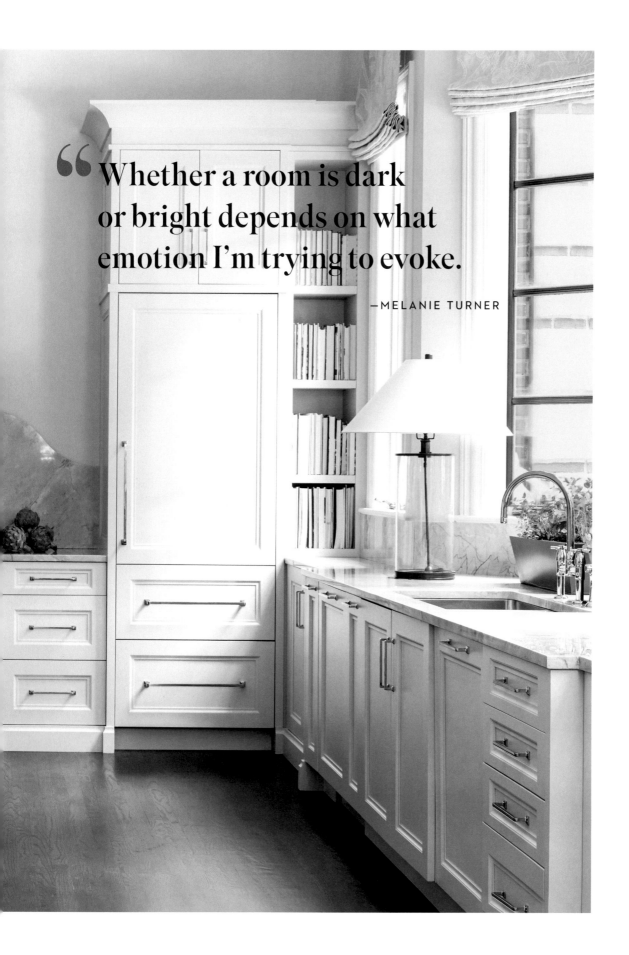

"Whether a room is dark or bright depends on what emotion I'm trying to evoke.

—MELANIE TURNER

blue and white forever

In demand and Insta-famous, designer
Mark D. Sikes knows what the people
want: gorgeous blues and their chic
counterpart, white. Now this Beverly
Hills family house wears his signature
palette from top to bottom.

The white kitchen's bold cobalt island, striped rugs, and patterned stools keep the white space from feeling too staid.

PRECEDING PAGES: Pops of black give the azure-splashed living room "a feeling of modernity," Sikes says.

Blue tassels embellish a white sofa in a corner of the living room. "Blue and white is a happy, timeless combination," Sikes says. "You can bank on it—it's a universal love."

Sikes cozied up the upstairs sitting room with inky fabric
on the walls and a sectional for TV watching.

5

TROPICS AND SUNSHINE

······················

Bring on the heat. These warm-weather havens have a sun-kissed glow, plenty of palms, and paradise pools for all-day lounging. Just add cocktails.

Sunlight pours into a Bahamian kitchen that's adorned head to toe with handmade cement tiles and coordinating lagoon-blue cabinetry with old-fashioned bin pulls.

life aquatic

The turquoise hues of the Bahamian waters reappear inside a Midwestern family's island getaway on Guana Cay. Designers Marshall Watson and Kate Reid zero in on shades of sand and surf for a tropical palette with a sense of place.

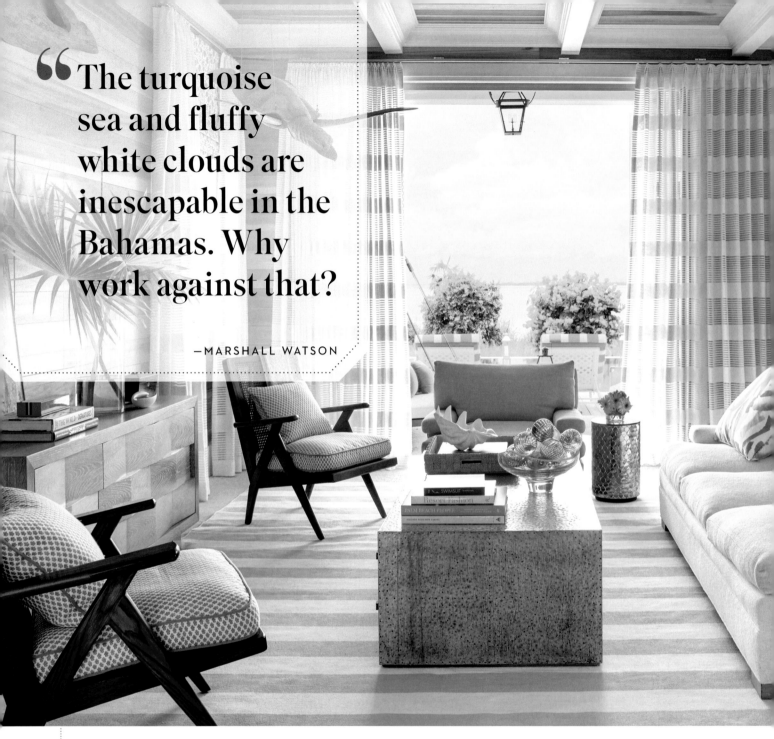

> # "The turquoise sea and fluffy white clouds are inescapable in the Bahamas. Why work against that?
>
> —MARSHALL WATSON

Raw poplar ceilings temper the chill-out blues in the living room. Stripes on the ethereal white curtains echo the coastline, and crisp white moldings keep things polished.

PRECEDING PAGES: A chippendale railing and gas lanterns embellish the rear façade of this British Colonial–style house. The designers spent hours matching the pool's glass mosaic to the color of the nearby ocean.

TOP RIGHT: A lamp and mirror, découpaged with shells and coral, appear in a hallway vignette. Watson and Reid used turquoise throughout the home but in different values from light to dark.

BOTTOM RIGHT: With no other place to put a powder room, the designers tucked it under the stairs behind a swinging bookcase. The painted map by the stairs includes the family's favorite local haunts.

picture perfect

Two stories provide twice the views of the sparkling Gulf waters at a beachfront cottage near Seaside, Florida. To add age beyond its years, Tammy Connor brought in loads of antiques, natural textures, and light-catching glass for a family getaway ready for memory-making.

PRECEDING PAGES: An eclectic assortment of vintage wicker looks cohesive on the screened-in porch when they're all painted the same deep-ocean blue. Views of the waves beyond remain unspoiled.

Another creative illumination trick appears in the guest bedroom, where vintage hurricane lanterns act as sconces. The recycled timber in the bed frame looks just as wind-scoured as the driftwood outside.

Pale oak floors and plank cabinetry with old-time latches give the kitchen a scrubbed look. The butcher block countertops exude warmth and informality.

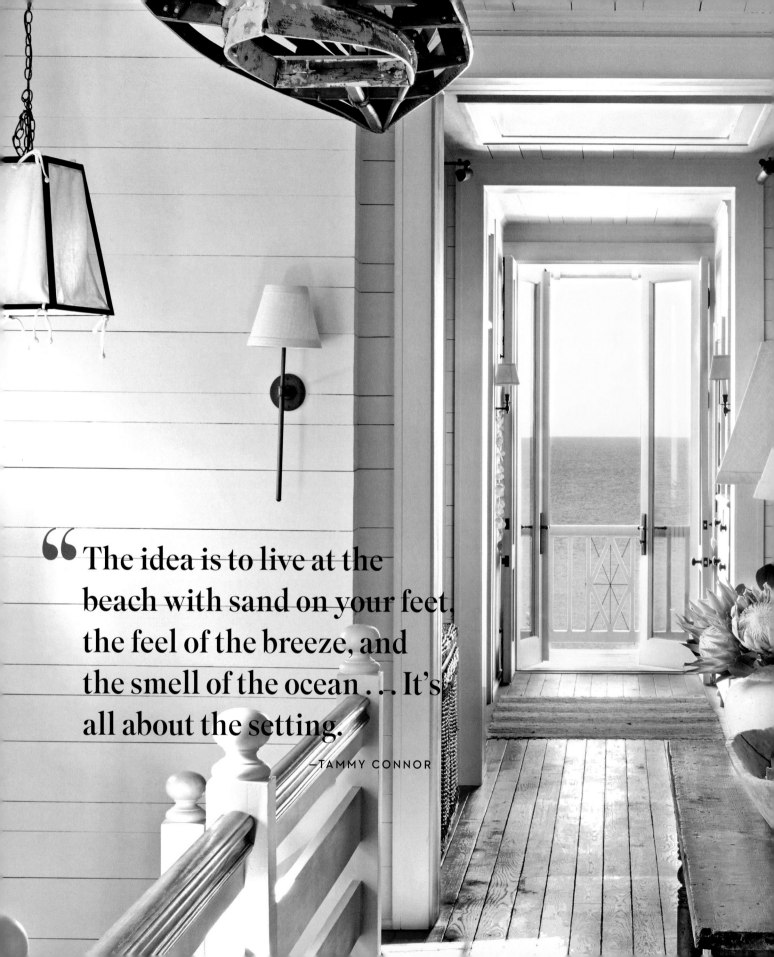

> " The idea is to live at the beach with sand on your feet, the feel of the breeze, and the smell of the ocean . . . It's all about the setting.
>
> —TAMMY CONNOR

Lamps made out of old amethyst-glass wasp catchers light up the "family memory wall." Connor bought $5 pictures at antiques shops just for the frames to create the sense that the collection grew over time.

not-so southern belle

Outdoor living comes easy in a new Beaufort, South Carolina, home outfitted with double porches and a classical courtyard. Peer inside and the open floor plan tells a different story, with all the urban glamour of the owners' former New York loft.

A mature palmetto lends shade and permanence to the recently built home, located in a historic district filled with eighteenth- and nineteenth-century residences. Fig ivy softens the back wall enclosing the outdoor sitting area.

Designer Michelle Prentice and her husband, photographer Josh Gibson, created a central courtyard by building the home in a U-shape. The patio chairs feature the same paint as the brick exterior.

The master bedroom's neutral palette reflects the color scheme throughout the house. Prentice added plenty of mirrored surfaces so the space "sparkles so much at night, it feels lit by candlelight."

On the second-floor veranda, a swing provides an idyllic reading spot overlooking a one-hundred-year-old oak. Gibson built the hanging daybed, inspired by the ones at Georgia's Greyfield Inn, where he and Prentice honeymooned.

"Neighbors walking by will see us inside, stop in to say hello, and we'll all wind up in the courtyard for a glass of wine.

—MICHELLE PRENTICE

“Gutsy moves gave each room its own stand-alone personality.

—ANDREW HOWARD

swimming in blues

"I'm going to reveal a professional secret about blue-and-white rooms," says Andrew Howard. "The truth is that they're impossible to mess up." That foolproof palette proved key when he took on a Ponte Vedra, Florida, home belonging to a fearless client who turned the classic color scheme on its head.

Sisal wallpaper "acts like a breather" in the dining room, Howard says. A pair of lanterns overhead feel less formal than a traditional chandelier.

PRECEDING PAGES: Howard inverted the usual paint plan by coloring the living room's walls white and its trim blue. The Moroccan tiles on the fireplace surround shine as "the star of the room," according to the designer.

Navy hues reign supreme in a guest bedroom with floral wallpaper. Howard tempered quirky touches throughout the house with classic elements like neutral sisals, wools, and timeless moldings.

Wicker armchairs pull together the look in the dining area on the porch. Cotton-linen pillows plush up the banquette.

sunny soul

With its cream-colored stucco façade and sumptuous gardens, a 1934 Spanish Colonial Revival in Richmond, Virginia, would look equally at home in Santa Barbara or Boca Raton. Lili O'Brien and Leigh Anne Muse let the dark wood and pale walls guide the way for an East Coast home with a Mediterranean heart.

The kitchen's 1850s English refectory table now functions as an island. O'Brien kept the wall a neutral color because "I have never seen a stucco wall inside an authentic Mediterranean house painted anything but cream, and I wasn't about to mess with that tradition."

A massive limestone fireplace presides over the living room. Gold glints on the Argentine mirror and custom coffee table, with marble and iron added for contrast.

A garden wall lush with climbing roses partitions off the pool area.

The master bedroom's balcony looks out onto the gardens and poolhouse. The late Richmond garden designer Charles Gillette created the elaborate boxwood parterres.

"I love the weighty feel of this house ... Everything has an artisanal hand.

—LILI O'BRIEN

island life

Pecky cypress, cement tiles, vintage rattan, batiks: Tom Scheerer drew on all his favorite "Bahama-isms" for a traditional Caribbean Colonial on Harbour Island, but with new life breathed in. To him, it's all about "finding a new melody with well-known notes."

The veranda's table has a travertine top on a teak base. "It can stay outside forever," Scheerer says. He chose bathing suit–friendly indoor/outdoor fabrics for the wicker seating's cushions as well as all the interior furniture.

A stroll down from the house leads to picture-perfect sands and sea.

The villa and pool located on the Dunmore property face the island's renowned Pink Sand Beach.

The pecky cypress in the foyer, one of Scheerer's favorites, repeats throughout the house. Vintage prints of sea life on the stair hall's back wall flank an extra-tall mirror that spans both floors.

Handmade cement tiles cover the kitchen backsplash, with "impermeable" porcelain on the floor. Metal fittings in a pewter finish can resist the tropical climate.

> **The best decorating always has a fillip of spontaneity, but on an island in the Bahamas, you have to plan ahead!**
>
> —TOM SCHEERER

A giant clamshell became a dramatic sink in the powder room.

Twin beds upholstered with the same purple ikat can be pushed together to become one—"though I've never met a middle-aged couple who didn't secretly relish a few nights in twin beds!" Scheerer jokes.

In the living room, a custom pickled teak-and-marble table, loaded with interesting finds, serves as the focal point. Scheerer positioned comfortable upholstery at the edges of the space, with more lightweight rattan and wicker toward the center.

palm beach bound

Designing her parents' dream home in Palm Beach, Sara Gilbane paid homage to their New England roots but added a little Floridian flair. Pecky cypress "beadboard" and plenty of blues (this time with coral and mango!) draw on the best of both worlds.

Visible from the most central part of the house, the kitchen had to marry style and function. A ladder provides built-in access to the upper cerused-oak cabinets.

Lively prints on the living room's custom club chair and ottoman mimic the antique tile on the fireplace surround. Gilbane calls the space's vibe "a Bahamas–meets–Palm Beach air."

FOLLOWING PAGES: An abstract painting by Simeon Braguin (left) plays into the living room's palette of faded blues and melons. The patterned rug masks the trails of sandy feet that traipse through the central space.

On the lawn, Gilbane chose outdoor seating with attached sailcloth canopies for shaded afternoon reading and evening cocktails.

An outdoor banquette on the loggia overlooks a garden only about ten feet from the Intracoastal Waterway, plus the nearby pool.

A spiky artichoke lamp nods to the bespoke wallpaper in a guest bedroom.

6

CHARMED!

A storybook ending is always in store at these enchanting hideaways, straight out of a fantasy. Some dreams really do come true.

The design of a newly built home in North Carolina's Blue Ridge Mountains was inspired by an aging barn and outfitted with old-house quirks, such as a closet for timber tucked into the chimney.

serenity now

A Swedish-American
family finds their bliss in a
quintessential Scandinavian
summer house, located on
an archipelago outside of
Stockholm. Marshall Watson
draws on shades of the sea and
sky for a retreat where the sun
seemingly never sets.

Watson carefully studied local architecture before reimagining the guesthouse, adapting the staircase's cut-out railings from other cottages in the area.

FOLLOWING PAGES: Cream, green, and pomegranate red run through the main house. Swedish Rococo chairs surround the dining room's custom-made table, while the long banquette by the window offers a cozy spot to read.

Steeply pitched rooflines in the master bedroom inspired Watson to use trellis-patterned panels. A simple desk in one of the window bays overlooks the Baltic Sea.

In the compound's guesthouse, foggy blues and soft grays make for a tranquil space. An antique settee pulls out to turn into a bed—the Swedish version of a convertible sofa.

66 The whole idea
is to invite more
light into a room.

—MARSHALL WATSON

sleepaway camp

A backyard campground brings back a burst of nostalgia when outfitted to perfection. Architect Steve Hoedemaker and designer Tim Pfeiffer of Hoedemaker Pfeiffer pitched a smattering of tents on the Seattle outpost of Whidbey Island, and they're definitely something to write home about.

Connected with bluestone pavers, the tents look out on a central fire pit. Extended flaps protect against sun and rain, while screened windows let cross breezes in.

The tented bedrooms in the Puget Sound retreat can accommodate dozens of guests at once. Canvas duck stretched over stained-oak rafters shields the plank floors.

A former cottage on the property now serves as an indoor gathering place.
The "mess hall" features half-log pine benches and 250-year-old Welsh chairs.

Cleanup is a group effort at the five-foot-long trough sink.
Artificial aging gave the exterior cedar shingles a weathered finish.

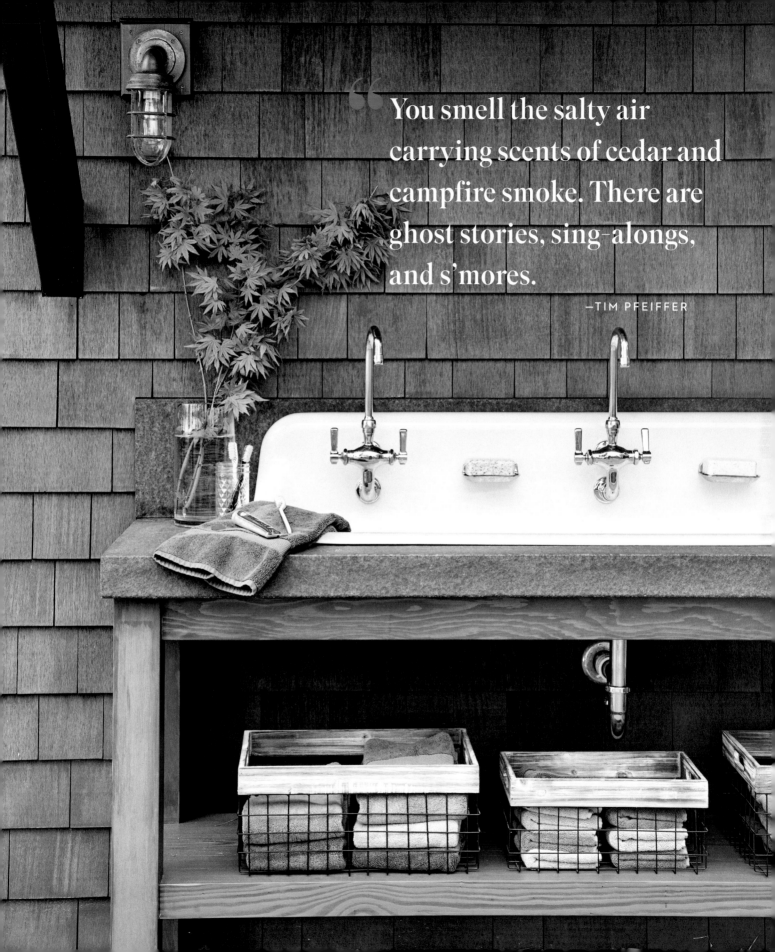

> "You smell the salty air carrying scents of cedar and campfire smoke. There are ghost stories, sing-alongs, and s'mores.

—TIM PFEIFFER

raising the barn

Age is just a number when it comes to a brand-new North Carolina retreat that embraces quirky old-house details. Architect James Carter teamed up with interior designer Jane Hawkins Hoke to create spaces both snug and substantial, with all the charisma one would expect of an alpine country house.

"When you enter, it feels like a tiny cottage," Carter says of the cozy foyer. "We wanted to delay the drama of the great room." The up-and-down stair landing creates the sense that the home's footprint grew over time.

A screened-in porch became a three-season space, thanks to the outdoor fireplace. A reproduction dovecote hangs on the wall of local stone.

PRECEDING PAGES: Built to resemble a converted barn, the great room utilized reclaimed wood and local stone for extra authenticity. Hoke selected oversize fabrics and furniture to stand up to the twenty-five-foot ceilings.

A closet in the chimney adds both whimsy and storage for firewood and furniture. The terrace's Adirondack chairs feature the same paint as the exterior trim.

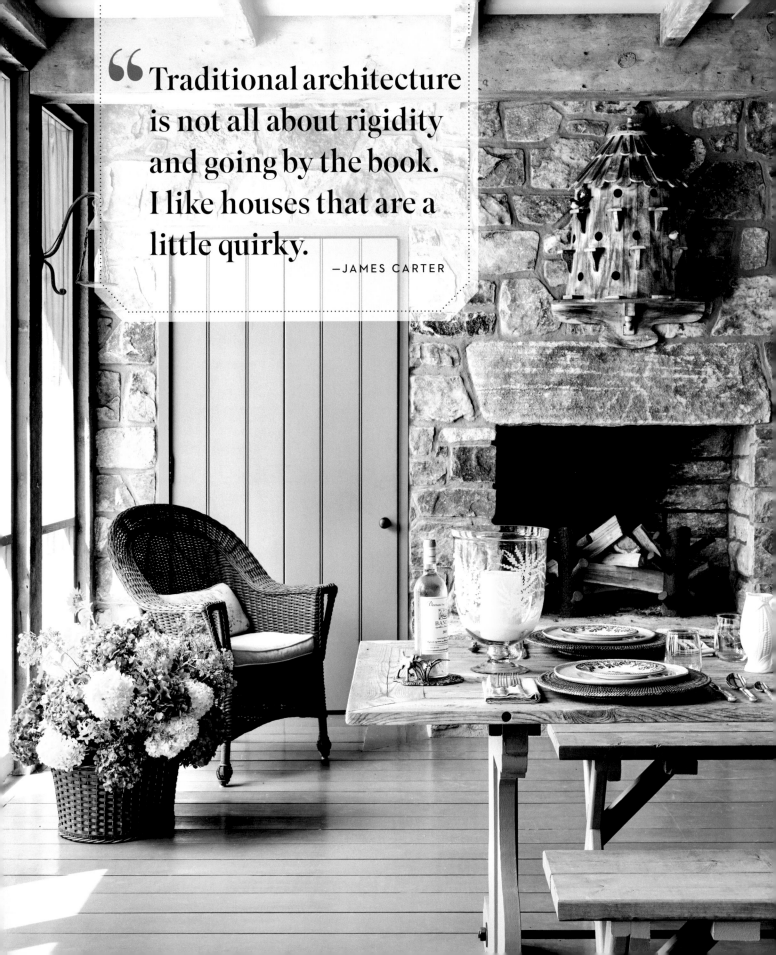

> "Traditional architecture is not all about rigidity and going by the book. I like houses that are a little quirky.

—JAMES CARTER

rock solid

Repurposing local fieldstone into an outpost of buildings, Wendy Owen created her own slice of southern France right in Sonoma—complete with pavilions for gardening, entertaining, and coffee drinking.

Outside the master suite, creeping fig and a small pond encircle the courtyard. Hydrangeas that turn chartreuse in the summer inspired the chaises' vibrant sphere pillows.

Provençal lavender scents the fields surrounding the potting shed, which also hosts girlfriends for tea. Owen added an old garden trowel to the weathered door as a knocker.

> "My aesthetic is very much about bringing the outdoors in.

—WENDY OWEN

An outdoor room in Saint-Paul-de-Vence, France, inspired this three-sided lounge pavilion. Owen made light fixtures from beehives and straw, a favorite with the swallows.

On the breakfast patio, French café chairs and a stone table overlook the nine-acre property and its century-old olive trees.

{ 219 }

cool as ice

Tucked in the attic of a Reykjavík
rowhouse, a seasonal pied-à-terre
keeps it chill. Brian Patrick Flynn
now ditches Atlanta's sweltering
summers for Iceland's snow and
sweater weather, staying in a sleek
pad with a glacial palette.

> **"Continuous pattern and dark colors make it about the mood, not the size.**

—BRIAN PATRICK FLYNN

An oversize table distracts from a niche's steeply pitched ceilings, while the cutwork base maintains airiness. Add an armless banquette, and the corner now works as a home office and lounge.

PRECEDING PAGES: Photographer Robert Peterson's portrait of a wind-blown Icelandic horse inspired this casually sophisticated living room. Flynn installed a wood beam on the ceiling for "instant architecture."

Tartan on the kitchen chairs pops against glossy white floors and bare windows. Ditching half the cabinets opened up the space for mini dinner parties.

A sleeping berth under a skylight offers guests views of the northern lights come winter.

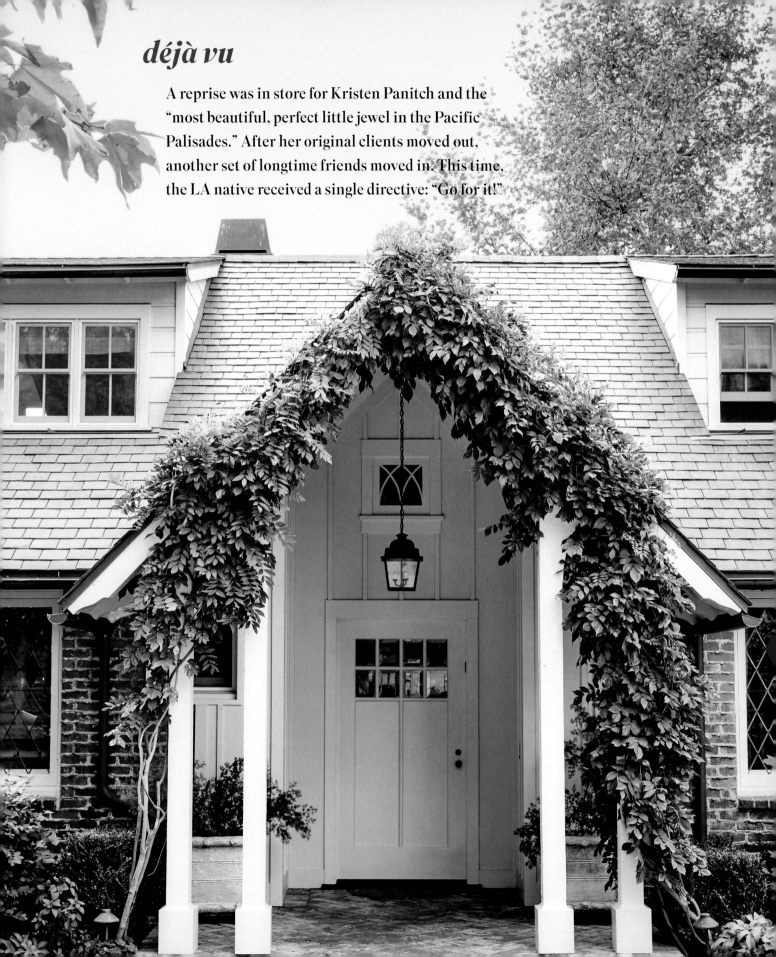

déjà vu

A reprise was in store for Kristen Panitch and the "most beautiful, perfect little jewel in the Pacific Palisades." After her original clients moved out, another set of longtime friends moved in. This time, the LA native received a single directive: "Go for it!"

Panitch skipped a rug in the dining room to avoid stuffiness. "I would rather spend money on the rugs you actually walk on," she adds. A small floral pattern on the chairs hides inevitable spills, and complements a kaleidoscopic wallpaper.

The character of the 1950s Arts and Crafts–style house comes courtesy of an ivy-draped portico and diamond window muntins.

> ❝ To create a
> sense of ease at
> home, surround
> yourself with
> what you love.
>
> —KRISTEN PANITCH

Panitch drew on English and Indian influences for the master bedroom covered with feather-patterned paper. The brass buttons on the tufted headboard feel "less fussy" than upholstered ones.

Reclaimed French-oak herringbone floors line the kitchen, with a white-tile backsplash to match. Custom leather stools sidle up to the island.

storybook ending

Set on grounds with weeping willows
and a swan-filled pond, an aging Atlanta
cottage found a renewed sense of fantasy
in the hands of Shon Parker. Added
beams and paneling, reconfigured
rooms, and newly installed 1920s steel
casement windows kick off a captivating
chapter in the home's history.

Rich walnut paneling lengthens the entryway's low ceilings. Parker replaced floral carpeting with marble tiling in a herringbone pattern.

With a steep roofline and swooping gables, the 1915 English-style cottage has a romantic feel. The owner chose to keep the moss growing over the weathered brick.

"Please yourself, not the imaginary person who might buy your house in the future.

—SHON PARKER

Darkened and waxed ceiling beams unify spaces throughout the house, including the guest bedroom.

An original Victorian cast-iron mantelpiece remains the library's crown jewel. Parker separated the space from the adjacent bedroom with a silk curtain, and added a geometric wallpaper up above.

into the blue

The entire crew comes aboard a Nantucket cottage pre- and post-regatta at the request of Gary McBournie's sailing-obsessed clients. With the party venue perched literally over the water, this charming boathouse is just as enticing as the yacht.

A stocked bar cart brings the party outside. "Imagine sitting out on the deck with a vodka tonic in the golden afternoon light," McBournie says. "You'll fall in love with the place."

FOLLOWING PAGES: Pennants from past races flutter over the living room. White beadboard and polished wood mix the rustic and the refined.

Extra guests squeeze onto the banquette for dinner. The cushions' polished duck cotton matches the sky and matchstick blinds connect the wood ceiling and floor.

Decks on three sides make the shingled wharf shack feel larger than its minimal footprint. McBournie painted the front door a welcoming nautical blue.

> "If you gussy up a place too much, you lose its character.

—GARY MCBOURNIE

RESOURCES

These designers, manufacturers, distributors, and retailers are featured throughout. *To the trade* (T) means a manufacturer sells primarily to design professionals.

PAINT

BENJAMIN MOORE, benjaminmoore.com

FARROW & BALL, farrow-ball.com

PORTOLA PAINTS & GLAZES, www.portolapaints.com

SHERWIN WILLIAMS, sherwin-williams.com

FABRIC & WALLCOVERING

BRUNSCHWIG & FILS (T), brunschwig.com

COWTAN & TOUT (T), cowtan.com

DE GOURNAY, degournay.com

DESIGNERS GUILD (T), designersguild.com

DURALEE (T), duralee.com

GRACIE (T), graciestudio.com

KRAVET (T), kravet.com

LEE JOFA (T), leejofa.com

PHILLIP JEFFRIES (T), phillipjeffries.com

QUADRILLE (T), quadrillefabrics.com

SCALAMANDRÉ (T), scalamandre.com

SCHUMACHER (T), fschumacher.com

SUNBRELLA (T), sunbrella.com

TULU, tulutextiles.com

FURNISHINGS & ACCESSORIES

1STDIBS, 1stdibs.com

B. VIZ DESIGN, bviz.com

BUNNY WILLIAMS HOME, bunnywilliamshome.com

CIRCA LIGHTING, circalighting.com

HARBINGER, harbingerla.com

HICKORY CHAIR (T), hickorychair.com

JOHN ROSSELLI ANTIQUES, johnrosselliantiques.com

JONATHAN ADLER, jonathanadler.com

LEONTINE LINENS, leontinelinens.com

MATOUK, matouk.com

MERIDA, meridastudio.com

NICKEY KEHOE, nickeykehoe.com

RALPH LAUREN HOME, ralphlaurenhome.com

RESTORATION HARDWARE, rh.com

SAMUEL & SONS (T), samuelandsons.com

SERENA & LILY, serenaandlily.com

STARK (T), starkcarpet.com

THE URBAN ELECTRIC CO., urbanelectricco.com

VISUAL COMFORT (T), visualcomfort.com

KITCHEN & BATH

LA CORNUE, lacornueusa.com

WATERWORKS, waterworks.com

WOLF, subzero-wolf.com

DESIGNERS

ANTHONY BARATTA, anthonybaratta.com

COLLEEN BASHAW, colleenbashaw.com

JEFFREY BILHUBER, bilhuber.com

MARTYN LAWRENCE BULLARD, martynlawrencebullard.com

MATTHEW CARTER, matthewcarterinteriors.com

TAMMY CONNOR, tammyconnorid.com

MARK D. SIKES, markdsikes.com

FRANK DE BIASI, frankdebiasi.com

TILTON FENWICK, tiltonfenwick.com

BRIAN PATRICK FLYNN, flynnsideout.com

SARA GILBANE, saragilbaneinteriors.com

RAMSAY GOURD, ramsaygourd.com

JANET GRIDLEY, janetgridley.com

JANE HAWKINS HOKE, 205-879-3406

ANNE HEPFER, annehepfer.com

HOEDEMAKER PFEIFFER, hoedemakerpfeiffer.com

ANDREW HOWARD, andrewjhoward.com

ANGIE HRANOWSKY, angiehranowsky.com

SHELLEY JOHNSTONE PASCHKE, shelleydesign.com

JOE LUCAS, lucasstudioinc.com

KATHRYN M. IRELAND, kathrynireland.com

MICHAEL MAHER, michaelmaherdesign.com

GARY MCBOURNIE, gmcbinc.com

JANIE MOLSTER, janiemolster.com

LILI O'BRIEN & LEIGH ANNE MUSE, obrienandmuse.com

MATTHEW O'DORISIO, mattodorisio.com

WENDY OWEN, wendyowendesign.com

KRISTEN PANITCH, kristenpanitchinteriors.com

SHON PARKER, shonparker.com

JOHN PEIXINHO, franklinandcompany.com

MICHELLE PRENTICE, prenticeinteriors.com

FRANK ROOP, frankroop.com

MELISSA RUFTY, melissarufty.com

TOM SCHEERER, tomscheerer.com

JILL SHARP WEEKS, jillsharpstudio.com

SARA STORY, sarastorydesign.com

SUMMER THORNTON, summerthorntondesign.com

MELANIE TURNER, melanieturnerinteriors.com

REBECCA VIZARD, bviz.com

MARSHALL WATSON, marshallwatsoninteriors.com

BARBARA WESTBROOK, westbrookinteriors.com

ASHLEY WHITTAKER, ashleywhittakerdesign.com

PHOTOGRAPHY CREDITS

ABOUT THE AUTHOR

CAROLINE PICARD is currently an editor at GoodHousekeeping.com and previously was an editor and writer for HouseBeautiful.com. She's a graduate of the Medill School of Journalism at Northwestern University. She lives in New York City.

INDEX

HEARSTBOOKS

An Imprint of Sterling Publishing Co., Inc.
1166 Avenue of the Americas
New York, NY 10036

ISBN 978-1-61837-283-3

Distributed in Canada by Sterling Publishing Co., Inc.
c/o Canadian Manda Group, 664 Annette Street
Toronto, Ontario M6S 2C8, Canada
Distributed in the United Kingdom by GMC Distribution Services
Castle Place, 166 High Street, Lewes, East Sussex BN7 1XU, England
Distributed in Australia by NewSouth Books
University of New South Wales, Sydney, NSW 2052, Australia

For information about custom editions, special sales, and premium and corporate purchases,
please contact Sterling Special Sales at 800-805-5489 or specialsales@sterlingpublishing.com.

Manufactured in China

2 4 6 8 10 9 7 5 3 1

sterlingpublishing.com
housebeautiful.com

Cover and interior design by Lorie Pagnozzi
Photography credits on page 237